Cryptocurrency

Advancing Past Fundamentals: Exclusive Approaches
And Methodologies To Achieve Prosperity As An Investor
And Trader In The Cryptocurrency Market

(The Intelligent Cryptocurrency Investor)

Howard Ferguson

TABLE OF CONTENT

Introduction	1
Cryptocurrency Investment Approach	15
Cryptocurrency Trading Strategies	35
Hacking Case Studies	54
How To Ensure The Longevity Of Cryptocurrency Investments	75
Factors To Consider Prior To Investing In Bitcoin	101
The Existing Condition Of The Market	106
Understanding Blockchain Technology	116

Introduction

As the dynamics of trading participants evolve over time, the methods by which global markets compensate for these transactions also undergo transformation. Over the course of the past five decades, the United States dollar (USD) has emerged as the dominant currency, serving as a catalyst and essential component of the global marketplace for commerce and assistance. It has served as the global reserve currency and has maintained a consistently high intrinsic worth. Henceforth, it is customary to observe that international transactions are consistently denoted in the currency of the United States. However, this was not consistently true. The subject of the extensive historical background is beyond the purview of this book. Nevertheless, it is crucial to note that the ascendance of the dollar in its significance occurred gradually over time due to global political factors. It did not always hold the status of being the global medium of exchange.

In order to acquire a more comprehensive grasp of the role and evolution of currency, it becomes imperative to comprehend that past transactions were primarily executed through personal interactions or entrusted messengers, documented on parchment or paper. The payment for the purchase was made in gold, or alternatively, it was exchanged through barter and subsequently converted into dollars.

But times have changed. Our dependency on bulk transactions has diminished compared to previous times, due to the increasing liberalization of the international trade market. Additionally, individuals possess the capacity to independently engage in cross-border transactions and promptly receive their purchases, regardless of their place of residence.

When considering entities such as Amazon in the United States and AliExpress in China, one can observe the extensive range of commodities that can be purchased, traded, and subsequently transported to any destination across the globe. This alteration significantly impacts the entirety of the financial transaction sector. In bygone times, it was only feasible to visit the vendor situated at the community's town square to conduct your purchase. He replenished his shelves by procuring goods from a nearby distributor, who sourced their inventory from a regional distributor, who in turn sourced their supply directly from the manufacturer or the importer. The importer would have consolidated the demand and executed a wholesale procurement from the overseas manufacturer. Upon such occurrence, the importer would proceed to the bank and initiate the establishment of a trade instrument, thereby facilitating the payment for the purchase to the seller. At this juncture, the banking institution would come into play by venturing into the financial markets to procure the necessary currency on behalf of the client.

Now, it is worth recalling that in the contemporary global landscape, a mere 1% of the transactions within the foreign exchange sphere can be categorized as transactional. An inherent issue arises from this practice as it engenders volatile fluctuations in the currency's value. There would be limited and sporadic transactions, leading to significant volatility in the currency prices. You witnessed a similar phenomenon with the emerging Bitcoin in 2011. There are two key concepts within this context that it is advisable for you to acquaint yourself with, as they will be recurrently employed throughout the duration of this book. The initial concept is referred to as "liquidity," while the second term is known as "volatility."

Neither of the terms are as obscure as they might initially seem, and the concept is intimately related to the word. Volatility illustrates the extent of fluctuations that can occur over time. When a commodity is referred to as volatile, it exhibits significant fluctuations and substantial price movements even with minimal transactions.

Conversely, liquidity refers to the asset's capacity to be readily traded without delay or difficulties. For example, consider a scenario where the market lacks liquidity. This implies that if I were to approach the market with the intention of purchasing USD, and there were no individuals willing to sell, I would be obliged to remain patient until a seller became available. Under those circumstances, in the event that there are no sellers available, yet I find myself in a position of urgency, my only recourse would be to present an offer at an elevated price. Subsequently, I would be compelled to progressively increase my proposition until an individual is inclined to vend me the Canadian dollar (CAD) presuming that I desire to remunerate my Canadian merchant with United States dollars (USD). In markets characterized by low liquidity, greater price fluctuations (volatility) arise due to the necessity of continually escalating my offer in order to attract sufficient interest for a transaction to occur.

This poses a significant challenge in the realm of global finance. Initially, there is an avoidable time lag, and additionally, there is a lack of consistency in currency valuations. This is the primary role that individuals such as yourself and I fulfill within the overarching framework of the market system. In order to maintain a continuous flow of transactions throughout the day, it is necessary for more than 80% of the total daily volume of transactions to be present, ensuring the availability of both a willing buyer and seller at any given time.

These traders willingly assume the potential consequences of fluctuations in prices and receive substantial compensation in return for their risk-taking. Additionally, they perform an invaluable and essential role within the global finance market by ensuring a stable and low-volatility environment, while also enhancing market liquidity. When I enter any market presently and endeavor to purchase Canadian Dollars (CAD) using United States Dollars (USD), the transaction is swiftly executed as there is consistently a purchaser present to complete the transaction.

There exists an additional stratum that it is imperative for you to acquaint yourself with. This is referred to as the "market maker." The market maker assumes the role of accommodating your buying or selling needs, irrespective of the availability of a matching buyer or seller for the transaction. This is due to the fact that he is generating a specific level of profit from the market-making endeavor. He assumes the potential volatility associated with fluctuations in price, in exchange for the premium incorporated into the exchange rate, which you are required to pay. Conversely, you receive the benefit of a prompt transaction.

Market makers play a critical role in the foreign exchange domain as they bridge the divide between buyers and sellers, assuming temporary ownership of the currency in lieu of waiting for a buyer to emerge, even in a market with high levels of liquidity. They effectively address the irregularities and inconsistencies, and are generously compensated for their contributions.

What is the significance of this in the context of cryptocurrency trading? Due to the uniform nature of trade, encompassing both cryptocurrencies and traditional currencies, irrespective of their specific form or mechanism. A transaction holds its fundamental nature intact, irrespective of whether it is carried out for the exchange of livestock or currency notes.

As the global landscape shifts away from traditional paper-based transactions, there is a discernible trend towards the prevalence of electronic transactions. This transition is accompanied by notable improvements in efficiency, bestowing upon us greater swiftness and adaptability. The frequency at which global transactions presently transpire is astounding and would have been unimaginable even in the previous era.

The capacity of paper-based transactions to remain viable is gradually diminishing, while a demand for an alternative means of conducting transactions is becoming evident. This is the fundamental rationale behind the growing popularity of BTC and other cryptocurrencies. It is not a passing trend; rather, it is a reflection of the evolving framework of business transactions.

Cryptocurrencies possess an ability not achievable by the current configuration of traditional currency. Cryptocurrencies possess the capacity to transform any form of asset into a medium for transactions, thereby enabling subsequent transacting. We shall address this topic in subsequent discussions; however, at present, it is imperative to comprehend that cryptocurrencies are not merely digital representations of currency. The transition extends beyond the mere shift from physical to digital records; rather, it pertains to the inherent characteristics of the transaction, encompassing its expeditiousness and its imperviousness to risks, within the fresh paradigm of commerce.

Consider, for example, the undeniable fact that it requires a minimum of three to five days to complete a payment via check or eCheck. A minimum of three days is required for cash transfers, particularly in the case of cross-border transactions. It may require a period of three business days for the transaction to be processed. If a weekend is included, the elapsed time from the initiation date to the day of receipt can amount to approximately 5 to 6 days. A payment transaction involving Bitcoin typically takes approximately ten minutes to complete.

Half a century ago, in the absence of computer technology, it was deemed acceptable for the process of payment and debt advice to span over a period of one month or longer. The physical medium carrying such information was subject to the cumbersome task of traversing the vast expanse of the ocean before reaching its intended recipient. Consequently, the arrival of international payments within a matter of weeks was anticipated. However, such behavior is deemed inappropriate in contemporary society.

Fraud is another issue. In the context of financial transactions, considerable possibilities exist for fraudulent activities. There are instances of dishonored checks, counterfeit banknotes, and incidents involving counterfeit wire transfers. In the current rapid transactional climate, it is imperative that the velocity of transactions and the integrity of these transactions are never subject to any uncertainties. Due to the inadequate level of security measures in place, it is necessary for transaction participants to endure a waiting period until funds are duly confirmed, thereby resulting in a significant time delay. In Bitcoin transactions, the validation process typically occurs within a matter of minutes. This is a significant rationale to support the notion that fiat currency will gradually yield to a cryptocurrency framework.

Before delving into the examination of the advantages and characteristics of cryptocurrency trading, it is imperative that you comprehend the aforementioned elements.

Cryptocurrency Investment Approach

Cryptocurrency has emerged as a prevalent topic of discussion among a significant portion of investors who have traditionally relied on conventional investment approaches for stocks, shares, bonds, and the like, as it presents an opportunity for substantial financial gains. At this point, you should possess a comprehensive understanding of the reasons behind the widespread discussion surrounding this digital currency. This is due to the fact that my book, entitled "The Beginner's Guide on Cryptocurrency," has provided you with an elaborate account of the complete historical background of cryptocurrencies and the fundamental technological framework that contributes to its popularity.

Why can cryptocurrency be a good investment? What criteria should be considered when selecting a suitable cryptocurrency? What strategies can be implemented to mitigate the risk of making errors in cryptocurrency investments? What is the recommended method of securely storing the acquired cryptocurrency? You have previously acquired the necessary information to address these inquiries, courtesy of the beginner's guide on cryptocurrency. Now that you have gained a comprehensive understanding of the concept of cryptocurrency investment, we shall endeavor to delve into the various investment strategies associated with this digital currency.

Cryptocurrency Investment Strategy

The prudent choice to engage in the investment of cryptocurrency carries inherent risks and potential gains, given the inherent volatility of the crypto market that results in swift fluctuations in the valuation of digital coins. However, when one possesses the intellectual capacity to conduct a thorough analysis of the market by leveraging historical data, subsequently determining the most suitable cryptocurrency to allocate investments into, they are effectively formulating a strategic approach for designing an impeccable course of action. This procedure is commonly known as the Cryptocurrency investment methodology.

What is the recommended amount to allocate towards the selected cryptocurrency? How can I ascertain that I am selecting the optimal strategy to generate favorable profits with my cryptocurrency? What level of convenience is associated with converting my cryptocurrency into cash? What would be the most secure method of preserving my coins? Could you please advise me on the optimal timing to sell my coin? The following are inquiries that will commonly arise once the decision to invest in cryptocurrency has been made.

As stated in the preceding section, establishing well-defined objectives is crucial for investors, necessitating a deliberate determination regarding the subsequent actions to be taken upon acquiring a cryptocurrency, as well as the anticipated timeline for generating profits from said investment. Developing a systematic blueprint and discerning the optimal approach for investment are pivotal elements in the realm of cryptocurrency investment.

- Could you kindly provide information on the designated budget reserved for cryptocurrency?

- Do you possess specific justifications for allocating your funds towards cryptocurrency investments?

- Are you financially capable of absorbing the potential loss of the 'initial investment' in the event of failure?

- Are you seeking a long-term investment opportunity or are you interested in a more expedient return through short-term investment?

- Are you interested in retaining ownership of your cryptocurrency coins?

- Are you considering adopting a well-rounded investment strategy that encompasses multiple assets, or are you inclined towards focusing solely on each cryptocurrency individually?

If you have formulated your cryptocurrency investment approach by considering the responses obtained from posing the aforementioned inquiries to oneself, then commend yourself for being on the correct trajectory.

The long-term investment strategy is widely regarded as the most exemplary approach currently employed in the market due to its reduced level of risk and lower transaction fees, obviating the need for frequent trading.

Purchasing the appropriate cryptocurrency at the optimal moment may also be regarded as a key investment approach within the realm of digital currencies. Refrain from purchasing the cryptocurrency when the price is significantly elevated with the assumption that you can subsequently sell it the following day at a considerably more favorable price. Apologies, but cryptocurrency transactions operate differently due to the inherent unpredictability of the market. Strive to make purchases during periods of low pricing and exercise patience until the price rebounds. Short-term waiting periods should span at least one month, while long-term waiting periods should extend beyond six months.

One can also engage in the purchase of cryptocurrencies during periods of price stability, wherein the fluctuation in value is minimal, and the differential figure remains relatively low.

What are the potential advantages of selecting an appropriate investment strategy?

When one possesses conscious understanding of their actions and their underlying purpose, they will possess the confidence necessary to proceed with the subsequent actions that pave the way for greater and more substantial progress. In a similar vein, once you have meticulously selected an investment strategy that aligns with your financial standing and ambitions, you are inclined to witness anticipated and unanticipated advantages. These rewards serve as a source of motivation, prolonging your stay in the market beyond your initial expectations upon venturing into the domain of cryptocurrency.

The right investment strategy will follow the below-mentioned steps:

Formulating a strategic framework for establishing your investment portfolio.

Considering the allocation you have intended for investment in cryptocurrency, it will be necessary for you to carefully select the digital currency that aligns most effectively with your financial objectives. It is crucial to establish plausible profit projections and adjust one's capabilities accordingly. Examine the coin's price valuation and thoroughly review its historical performance in order to make an educated estimation in the volatile market, enabling you to develop a strategic plan for withdrawal at the appropriate time.

Do not hesitate to acknowledge the decline in price value.

Once you have made the decision to invest in cryptocurrency, it is essential to be mentally and financially prepared to acknowledge and embrace the fluctuating prices of various digital currencies in the market. The occurrence of these price dips is not arbitrary; you should be prepared to discern the underlying cause for these fluctuations. The subsequent elucidation could provide a couple of rationales for the regular decline in the value of prices:

- The appreciation in price of a specific cryptocurrency may result in the depreciation of another cryptocurrency, and vice versa.

- Speculation surrounding cryptocurrency in general or on a specific coin may also serve as a contributing factor.

- Publicized reports regarding cryptocurrencies, such as "Bitcoin's price surge causes Litecoin's decline," have the potential to incite individuals to flock towards Bitcoin, resulting in the panic-driven sale of Litecoins and consequently altering the value of both currencies.

- The acceptance or prohibition of cryptocurrencies in various nations can also exert influence on the cryptocurrency market landscape.

It is crucial to maintain composure and avoid becoming emotionally reactive in such situations.

Securing digital assets

Securing the digital assets in a secure location is a critical aspect in the realm of cryptocurrencies. Given that the currency exists solely in digital form and lacks tangible representation, it becomes increasingly crucial to identify a secure method of preserving its integrity. The coins must possess impervious security measures to safeguard against illicit activities such as cyber hacking, viral infiltration, malware intrusion, theft, and related risks that can compromise the integrity of stand-alone systems. In the conventional mode of transaction, should you misplace your Internet banking password, you can seek assistance from the bank to obtain a new password. In the event of your card being stolen, it is advisable to promptly get in touch with the authorized individual and request the immediate suspension of the card in order to curb any potential unauthorized transactions.

However, in the realm of cryptocurrencies, one does not possess any such alternatives. In the event of misplacing your private key, it encompasses the consequence of relinquishing access to your cryptocurrency holdings. They have departed! There exists no avenue through which they can be recovered. In the event that the cryptocurrency you had previously deposited in the web-based wallet has been unlawfully acquired, regrettably, there exists no feasible means by which you can recover your funds, owing to the anonymous nature of crypto transactions. In the event that you have mistakenly transferred your coin to an incorrect address, it will not be possible to retrieve it unless the recipient chooses to initiate a return. Therefore, it is crucial to ensure the secure storage of your cryptocurrency assets. This can be accomplished by utilizing a hardware wallet or paper wallet, maintaining a backup of the cryptocurrency's .dat file, implementing two-factor authentication, among other precautions."

Exemplification of a cryptocurrency investment approach

The return on investment for cryptocurrency has surged to an impressive 900% since the commencement of 2017. In contrast, attaining similarly substantial ROIs within the conventional stock market or equity market is exceedingly challenging. The long-term investment approach in cryptocurrency yields significant returns, and the magnitude of these gains is astonishing.

What constitutes a long-term investment strategy? In contrast to the conventional stock market, where a long-term strategy entails retaining shares for a duration of three years or more, the cryptocurrency market operates at an exceedingly accelerated pace, thereby reducing the waiting period to months or years. There have been instances wherein investors made a $200 investment in cryptocurrency coins in January and realized returns amounting to $2000 by the end of the year, or within a shorter timeframe.

Promising investment strategies to consider.

For Bitcoin

Utilizing the concept of 'purchasing downturns' in the realm of cryptocurrency can be regarded as a fundamental investment approach, referring to the acquisition of modest portions of Bitcoin during periods of the currency's reduced value, followed by the retention of said portions for a designated timeframe until their subsequent sale during a state of market stability. There are two approaches in which you can attempt to implement this strategy:

Purchase Bitcoin once the price stabilizes, meaning it may have experienced a recent decline followed by a gradual and consistent recovery.

- Continuously purchase fractional amounts of Bitcoin at consistent intervals every time the price decreases.

If you possess substantial investment expertise, you have the ability to 'establish purchase orders' by setting buy orders at prices below the prevailing market value, and subsequently allowing them to be executed.

There exist two classifications in the context of 'purchasing downturns':

- Purchase during minor market corrections (when the price declines from its previous value)

- Purchase stocks during significant market downturns (when prices decline substantially, falling well below the average level). - Capitalize on substantial decreases in stock prices (where prices experience a sharp decline, dropping significantly below the average level). - Take advantage of major price declines in the market (where prices plummet significantly, falling well below the average level). - Seize opportunities to buy stocks when they experience steep declines in price (where prices drop dramatically, falling below the average level).

When engaging in the purchase of significant decreases in value, one may adopt a 'buy and hold strategy' to establish a resilient long-term cryptocurrency portfolio. Alternatively, if one intends to engage in range trading, they may opt for acquiring minor decreases in value.

It is advised to solely engage in selling when the value of the price is elevated, without any alternative course of action. The optimal strategy is to acquire assets at a lower price and subsequently divest them at a higher valuation.

Recommendation: It is prudent to monitor the fluctuations in the value of Bitcoins over various time periods such as one hour, one week, one month, one quarter, and six months before determining the optimal time to engage in buying or selling transactions. It is also recommended to promptly initiate temporary pauses, known as "stops," whenever deemed necessary.

For Ether

Regarding Ether (ETH), it is recommended to adhere to the strategy of purchasing and retaining the asset for a prolonged duration. Allocate a modest sum towards the acquisition of the coin, exercising the patience to retain ownership of said coin for a predetermined duration, approximately one year. Once the opportune moment arises, you may opt to exchange the coin for another cryptocurrency or convert it into conventional currency, commonly referred to as 'fiat currency,' by selling it on a reputable cryptocurrency exchange.

- You have the option to utilize either 'Coinbase' or 'LocalEthereum' as platforms for purchasing Ether (ETH). - Both 'Coinbase' and 'LocalEthereum' are available to facilitate the acquisition of Ether (ETH). - The procurement of Ether (ETH) can be accomplished through the utilization of either 'Coinbase' or

'LocalEthereum'. - 'Coinbase' and 'LocalEthereum' present themselves as viable options for the acquisition of Ether (ETH). - For the purchase of Ether (ETH), you may consider either 'Coinbase' or 'LocalEthereum' as potential avenues.

Considering your allocated investment funds, the coin can be acquired.

After the completion of the coin purchase, one has the option to transfer the coin from an online wallet to an offline wallet or a hardware wallet for the purpose of secure storage.

If you have made the determination to defer for a duration of six months to one year, subsequently safeguard the coin during this period and maintain possession of it.

Upon the arrival of the designated time, you may opt to engage in the exchange of the aforementioned digital currency with an alternate crypto asset, or alternatively, liquidate said digital currency for conventional fiat currencies, contingent upon the prevailing market conditions.

CHAPTER SUMMARY:

This chapter will guide you through the following:

- Strategy for Investing in Cryptocurrencies - Cryptocurrency Investment Plan - Approach to Investing in Cryptocurrencies - Formal Cryptocurrency Investment Strategy - Methodology for Investing in Cryptocurrencies

The advantages of selecting an appropriate investment strategy

- A demonstration of a cryptocurrency investment approach

- Potential investment approaches applicable to Bitcoin and ether - Investment strategies suitable for utilization with Bitcoin and ether - Feasible investment tactics that can be implemented for Bitcoin and ether

"YOUR PROMPT INITIATING ACTION ITEM:

Although cryptocurrency can be an uncertain realm for novice and seasoned investors alike, it can undoubtedly yield substantial advantages when approached with prudence and caution. As an investor, it is imperative to proactively initiate the subsequent measures in order to gain a competitive edge in the market:

- Engage in activities that will ensure you remain well-informed about developments in the cryptocurrency market.

Engage with online communities and platforms dedicated to discussions on various cryptocurrencies including Bitcoin, Ethereum, Litecoin, Dash, and others. to comprehend the prevailing market valuation.

- Familiarize yourself with news articles discussing the potential risks associated with cryptocurrencies in order to gain insights into the presence of a market bubble.

Maintain composure at all times and refrain from engaging in impulsive selling of your cryptocurrency investments as a result of market volatility.

Cryptocurrency Trading Strategies

Similar to engaging in the trading of securities and forex, the act of trading in cryptocurrency necessitates the development and implementation of a thorough trading strategy. Having a well-defined strategy is crucial when engaging in any form of trade or investment, with cryptocurrencies being no different. Nonetheless, given the heightened instability and pervasive speculation observed in cryptocurrency markets, it becomes even more crucial to establish a comprehensive trading strategy for such assets.

What constitutes a trading plan?

A trading plan serves as a structural framework that allows individuals to articulate and delineate their trading endeavors. It encompasses a set of criteria, regulations, and principles that must be adhered to in the conduct of your business endeavors.

Although there is not a definitive template for a trading plan due to the individuality of each trader's needs, risk tolerance, and lifestyle, it is essential to take into account commonly acknowledged principles while formulating your trading plan.

Whose requirement is it to possess a trading plan?

Every trader is obligated to have a trading plan. Each and every trader requires a well-defined trading strategy. It is frequently asserted that as one gains expertise and broadens their knowledge in a particular profession, their dependence on a trading plan diminishes. This is a fallacy. It could denote that you have effectively assimilated your fundamental trading plan, obviating the need for continuous reference to it. Nevertheless, this indicates that you have surpassed the fundamental principles and, as a result, must enhance your trading strategy in order to elevate yourself as a more proficient trader operating at an elevated level.

Strategic trading blueprint – your navigational guide

A trading plan delineates one's trading goals and the methods they will employ to accomplish them. A trading plan serves as a navigational guide that charts your course from your current trading position to your desired destination of becoming a proficient trader.

In order to ascertain a lucid delineation of your trading plan, it is imperative that you pose these fundamental inquiries to yourself and offer corresponding elucidations: "

May I inquire about your present situation regarding your strengths, weaknesses, opportunities, and threats?

What is the timeframe within which you conduct your trading activities?

What is the extent of your knowledge and experience?

What are the specifics of your capitalization strategy?

What is your vision?

What is your goal?

What is your plan that has been adjusted for the appropriate timing?

What specific type of success do you aspire to attain?

A trading plan refers to a strategic business plan that has been customized to focus on the trading of a specific product (funnel).

Key principles governing the trading plan

Each plan is tailored to suit your specific requirements and inclinations. There lacks a universally applicable strategy or all-encompassing framework for execution. However, it is crucial to take into account the three essential guidelines mentioned below in designing your plan:

Please document your plan.

Record your progress

Control your risk

Key inquiries pertaining to trading strategy

One optimal approach to developing a comprehensive trading plan involves addressing pivotal inquiries. Please provide responses to the questions listed below within your trading plan:

What serves as the driving force behind your decision to engage in the trading industry? Is it:

To rapidly generate monetary funds with utmost expediency

To engage in the exhilarating endeavor of the emerging technology

To optimize revenue-generation prospects

To establish a viable economic livelihood

To expedite the growth of your retirement fund

What is the extent of your understanding regarding cryptocurrencies?

I am commencing my journey and require hands-on experience to acquire practical knowledge in trading.

I am relatively inexperienced in the field of cryptocurrency trading, however, I possess a strong ability to quickly acquire knowledge and adapt to new concepts.

I possess extensive expertise in specific aspects of cryptocurrency trading, however, there remain certain areas which require further elucidation.

I possess a comprehensive understanding of the cryptocurrency concept, including its market dynamics and trading strategies.

What level of risk are you willing to tolerate?

I prioritize safety and risk mitigation (preferring secure options).

I maintain a risk-neutral stance, carefully considering both risks and rewards.

I frequently engage in ventures involving substantial risk due to my preference for the attractive returns they offer.

How many hours are you able to allocate towards engaging in cryptocurrency trading?

I am fully committed to devoting my time to it, and am available to make it my primary occupation.

I am available to work part-time during my spare hours.

I can choose to pursue it as a recreational pastime, indulging in it only when I am in the appropriate disposition.

Formulating a strategic trading blueprint "

Trading plans are tailored to individual preferences. You have the ability to tailor your trading plan according to your individual preferences. Nevertheless, it is imperative to include specific fundamental elements. The subsequent points should be taken into account in order to establish a sound trading plan:

Familiarize yourself with your standing as a trader - this entails conducting a thorough self-assessment via SWOT Analysis.

Precisely articulate your objectives and align them consistently with each action and choice you undertake.

Please make a determination regarding whether you wish to pursue a short trading or a long trading position.

Determine your primary trading pairs and trading timeframes.

Develop your individualized trading methodology.

Determine the level of risk that is financially feasible for you.

Ascertain the approach through which you shall manage your ongoing trades.

Implement a comprehensive system for maintaining accurate records

Conduct a retrospective analysis of your trading system

Personal trading system

A trading system forms an integral component of a trading plan, which encompasses a well-structured sequence of steps to be undertaken in response to specific occurrences. This scheme has been formulated in accordance with a set of guidelines established by yourself. A trading system streamlines and automates your decision-making process, thereby reducing your vulnerability to psychological errors.

Nevertheless, this does not imply that it is mechanically inflexible. It is essential for it to possess the capacity for adjustment and adaptation to fluid market dynamics. However, this should not serve as a justification for you to behave in a capriciously discretionary manner. In order to prevent irrational judgments, it is advisable that any modifications made to your trading system undergo thorough testing to verify their effectiveness, credibility, and dependability.

A rudimentary trading system should encompass the following fundamental elements:

Trade signals - These are discernible circumstances that are sought in the market as cues for a likelihood of a profitable trade. Established signals consist of elevated peaks, reduced troughs, dynamic averages, etc. The choice of setup is contingent upon one's classification as either a short trader or a long trader.

Critical junctures – These are precise instances that necessitate strategic intervention based on predetermined arrangements. Triggers may be classified as either manual or automated, contingent upon the level of proficiency and the availability of the necessary tools within your trading platform. While the majority of forex markets are equipped with advanced set-up and trigger tools, a scant few cryptocurrency platforms possess such capabilities. Despite possessing these tools, they remain rudimentary in nature. Therefore, you are more inclined to depend on manual configurations and stimuli.

Conducting retrospective analysis on your trading system

Back-testing entails subjecting your trading system to a testing framework, wherein hypothetical or historical data is employed to ascertain its validity, reliability, and effectiveness. This holds substantial significance as it can assist you in preventing substantial financial losses attributed to dependence on a faulty trading system.

There are two alternatives available: you may conduct the back-testing process independently, or you have the option to enlist the services of skilled and professional back-testers to perform it on your behalf. Although cryptocurrencies and fiat currencies are generated using distinct systems and technologies, they are both underpinned by the fundamental principles of trading. Therefore, a foreign exchange back-testing framework can be employed to conduct back-tests on cryptocurrency trading systems with minimal modifications.

Risk management

Risk management is a critical and unavoidable element of a well-crafted trading strategy. Without the implementation of risk management strategies, it would be difficult to assert that you possess a comprehensive trading plan. The effective implementation of risk management is contingent upon the level of risk tolerance one possesses. It is also contingent upon whether you engage in short-term or long-term trades.

However, it is essential to establish a foundation for formulating your risk management strategy. The subsequent inquiries must be addressed in order to provide effective guidance for your risk management strategy:

What percentage of my account can I allocate as a potential risk for each trade?

What is the maximum number of trading positions I am prepared to manage simultaneously?

What is the highest degree of risk to which I am willing to expose my account?

Advantages of implementing a strategic trading plan.

It is evident that the implementation of a well-structured trading plan yields substantial advantages in the pursuit of successful trading. "However, it is important to emphasize the primary advantages that you can obtain from a well-designed trading strategy:

Methodical and efficient decision-making process

Streamlined and structured trading

Structured risk management

Established predetermined entry and exit strategies prior to initiating trades.

Efficient management of accounts and transactions

Key pitfalls to steer clear of

The manner in which you experience and react to your trading activities significantly impacts your decision-making. Occasionally, it has the potential to enhance or hinder one's capacity for decision-making. This phenomenon constitutes the psychological element present in all trades, cryptocurrency being no exception. It is imperative not to disregard the importance of your psychology when engaging in trading activities.

The primary cause of errors made in trading predominantly stems from psychological influences. It is imperative to have knowledge of such matters in order to establish command. Here is a compilation of prevalent errors attributed to psychological factors:

Incorporating emotional states into your decision-making process (e.g. fear, avarice, tension, delight, agitation, etc.)

Partaking in emotionally-driven trading

Being impatient

Being restless

Being indecisive

Being unprepared

Assuming easy profits

Over-relying on software

Poor timing

Failing to maintain documentation

Neglecting to evaluate the ratio between risk and reward.

Deviation from adherence to one's trading strategy

Choosing not to minimize your losses

Exhibiting an excessive response to your victory

Constraining your choices

The act of spreading one's resources or investments too thinly through over-diversification.

Excessive exposure

Engaging in unnecessary risk-taking.

Addressing Popular Misconceptions Regarding Current Trends

Trading plan tips

Be disciplined

Ensure that you stay on course with your advancements.

Stay rational

Do not permit psychological elements to overpower you.

Hacking Case Studies

Assailants purloined the sum of $500,000 in bitcoins from a cryptocurrency user: this incident occurred during the nascent stage of Bitcoin, when merchants had only recently begun to embrace bitcoins as a form of payment for their goods and services. Bitcoin did not enjoy widespread recognition during this period. And had not accomplished its current status. Even during that particular period, it exhibited the capacity to induce a state in which honey drew the attention of bees.

In early 2011. Bitcoin was predominantly recognized within the tech-savvy community. Not even famous ones. And confined to a select few among their ranks. One could depict it as an exclusive community comprised solely of individuals who possessed specialized knowledge and pursued various hobbies. During that period, cryptocurrency mining encountered lesser challenges due to reduced competition. Nobody will undertake the arduous task of solving intricate puzzles and complex mathematical functions for a meager sum. It can be inferred that Crypto Mining was considerably more manageable, to the point where it was viable even on personal computers. Individuals simply need to take a moment to engage in the process of solving a puzzle and subsequently acquire a substantial amount of cryptocurrency. Similar was the situation pertaining to an individual, whose identity shall remain undisclosed, as he maintained a consistent presence on a bitcoin forum and engaged in regular cryptocurrency mining activities.

Through a fortuitous combination of adeptness and expertise, he has successfully extracted a staggering *sum of 25,000 bitcoins since the inception of the bitcoin phenomenon. Now, allow me to inform you all that during the initial phase, the value of bitcoins was mere fractions of a cent. However, at the onset of 2011, its worth escalated to $20. Therefore, this individual successfully extracted bitcoins with a value amounting to $500,000. However, on the 13th of June, 2011, he experienced a significant loss of all his bitcoins as a result of an unspecified assault.*

The digital currency was securely held within a physical storage device. It is widely held, within the realm of consensus, that an individual with malicious intent infiltrated his personal computer and executed a transaction, transferring the entire balance of 25,000 BTC to an undisclosed and untraceable account. Now, what measures can be implemented? There is a lack of oversight from any authoritative entity to address disputes pertaining to crypto currencies, consequently resulting in a state where there is no recourse for resolution.

If those bitcoins were not subject to unauthorized access, their value today would amount to $250 million. The aforementioned incident occurred as a direct result of hackers gaining control of his personal computer and successfully accessing the hard drive. Thus, this did not constitute a software-related problem in which retracing steps is less complex. Once again, it becomes evident that since the inception of BTC, it has lacked inherent safety measures, thereby enabling hackers to exploit its untraceable nature.

A highly renowned wallet service has become defunct: A bitcoin wallet is being acquired by cryptocurrency users. When engaging in cryptocurrency mining, individuals require a digital wallet for the purpose of securely storing and accessing the mined coins. Bitcoin wallets are specifically designed wallets that facilitate the secure storage of bitcoins. An example of a wallet service provider was MyBitcoins. This particular bitcoin wallet provider garnered significant popularity during the initial stages of BTC; however, it suddenly ceased to exist without any forewarning or explanation, precisely in the month of August in 2011. The service provider, in an official statement, has confirmed that the aforementioned website was subject to a cyber attack, resulting in its removal from the internet.

Numerous incidents of this nature transpired, with even bitcoin wallets succumbing to unauthorized access by malicious individuals.

It is evident that neither BTC nor Bitcoin wallets are characterized by dependability.

It is analogous to the act of procuring or leasing a storage unit within a financial institution where one is aware of the existence of potential weaknesses. Nobody will engage in such behavior. This holds true in this situation as well. The security of the location where individuals store their cryptocurrency is also compromised. There is a lack of governing body to oversee them, nor can they be deemed trustworthy or assume accountability for any resulting losses. It is possible for situations to arise in which bitcoin wallet service providers themselves engage in fraudulent activities. In certain instances, once they amass a substantial volume of BTC, they may abscond, attributing such actions to purported cyber attackers breaching their website's security. The proverb is straightforward and its narrative cannot be subjected to inquiry. All the painstaking efforts put into earning BTC through puzzle-solving and investing significant amounts of time and effort will ultimately render it devoid of value.

Interests and investments in BTC can result in a complete waste of time and a 100% loss of funds, as there exists no viable means of authenticating bitcoin wallets. Furthermore, it is impossible to ascertain the veracity of claims regarding hackers' attacks or discern whether they are part of a meticulously orchestrated fraudulent scheme.

Unlawfully access a communal network: The aforementioned occurrence transpired in March 2012. In this instance, assailants capitalized on vulnerabilities within the web hosting service known at that time as Linode. Several users of Linode had 46,703 bitcoins unlawfully retrieved by hackers. In reference to the aforementioned incident, a web platform known as Bitcoinica, which operated as an early bitcoin exchange, experienced a loss of 43,000 bitcoins. Such achievements were made feasible by virtue of the interconnected network. It is evident that in the present day, numerous gaps remain in network configurations, leading to vulnerabilities that facilitate unauthorized access to shared networks.

Thus far, it is evident that instances of hacking predominantly occur within public networks such as wifi or shared networks. Subsequently, in May of the same year, precisely within a span of two months, the aforementioned network fell prey to yet another assault by cybercriminals, resulting in the appropriation of 18,000 BTC from Bitcoinica. In order to address these attacks, Bitcoinica temporarily suspended its online operations and *conducted a comprehensive reassessment of all security-related matters. Despite an internal audit having been conducted, it was regrettably delayed until this point. Shortly thereafter, in August 2012, a multitude of Bitcoinica users expressed their discontent and initiated legal proceedings against the company. These individuals requested the reimbursement of an amount as significant as $460,000 in deposited funds. Bitcoincia succumbed to these circumstances and subsequently experienced a decline as a result of substantial financial losses. This entire sequence of events occurred solely due to the lack of attention towards security protocols in web and sharing networks. The gap that emerges during the process of network sharing may vary in magnitude, yet it will consistently provide ample opportunity for attackers to successfully exploit your bitcoin account.*

Chapter 2: An Analysis of the Pairs Trading Strategy

In the realm of finance, the theory of change posits that interest rates, encompassing security prices and economic indicators, will ultimately revert back to their historical average levels.

For instance, a considerable number of investors acquired shares of Infosys when the stock price experienced a significant decline subsequent to the resignation of CEO, Mr. Vishal Sikka. This action reflects their anticipation that the trading of Infosys stocks will witness an upsurge in the future, once the concerns related to the company's management are effectively addressed.

The principles of average return can be utilized when considering fundamental factors, such as the purchase of a stock with a low price-to-earnings (PE) ratio, with the expectation that the PE ratio will increase to align with the historical average PE ratio or the industry's average PE ratio.

Typically, the value investor adheres to this strategy when acquiring stocks for long-term investment purposes. By employing indicators, we can effectively implement these principles to develop trading strategies focused on short-term average reversion.

Meaning change strategy

The statistical arbitration strategy leverages the concept of semantic change to capitalize on the advantage of price volatility among a collection of securities. This particular trading strategy ranks among the most widely embraced approaches in the domain of quantitative trading. Various forms of statistical arbitrage trading strategies exist.

Directional trade

In the realm of directional trading, the signal emitted by each instrument remains detached from the signal produced by any other instrument.

For instance, there has been an increase in expenditure on the procurement of crude oil in the previous month. Unexpectedly, and without any significant catalyst or announcement, the expenditure allocated towards the procurement of crude oil undergoes a sudden alteration, resulting in a decrease to $20. Based on the principle of mean variation, a decrease in expenditure on crude oil acquisitions can be anticipated in the upcoming days. The mean alteration in expenditure on crude oil acquisitions remains constant, thereby presenting you with a favorable prospect to capitalize on.

Integrated portfolio trading

In this particular trading strategy, the generation of trading signals relies on the integration of two or more instruments. Pair trading is regarded as one of the most prevalent instances of this particular trading methodology.

As we employ two integrated instruments for trading, known as pair trading, it is noteworthy that the trading pairs may not always be restricted to two securities but can extend to triplets or even larger groupings. Should you come across a selection of five integrated stocks, you will have the opportunity to construct a portfolio and engage in trading activities.

This chapter will be dedicated to exploring the concepts of pairs trading and the accompanying strategies used in its execution.

Fundamental concepts of pair trading

Imagine possessing a set of instruments that are grounded in identical fundamental principles, pertaining to the same sectors, and exhibiting similar economic interconnections. Examples include stocks such as Google and Microsoft, or

Facebook and Twitter.

Given that their fundamental principles align, it is reasonable to anticipate that both stocks will exhibit equivalent behavior. Additionally, it is anticipated that the ratio or distribution of such stocks will remain consistent over an extended period. Nevertheless, variations in the distribution of pairs might arise as a consequence of transient fluctuations in supply and demand, alongside other pertinent factors.

In instances of this nature, one security demonstrates superior performance compared to the other. Based on the principle of average return, it is anticipated that this deviation will converge to its normal state gradually. In circumstances of temporal disparity, one may engage in pair trading. The process involves purchasing securities with lower performance levels and selling securities with higher performance levels.

Correlation vs. Cointegration

The majority of individuals perceive the correlation and cointegration as interchangeable. However, such is not the present circumstance.

When two price series demonstrate either a concordant or discordant trajectory, a correlation can be inferred between the two. In the event that one series of prices experiences upward or downward movements, correspondingly leading the second series of prices to exhibit the same trajectory, it indicates a positive correlation.

If the direction of one price series demonstrates an upward or downward movement, the other exhibits a corresponding movement in the opposite direction, indicating a negative correlation between the two series.

Cointegration is a statistical characteristic of a set of two or more price series, which implies that if a linear combination of the series is stationary, then the two series are linked.

For example, when the linear combination of two stocks remains constant, it can be inferred that there is a connection between the two stocks. A price series is deemed static if it remains consistent and experiences no variations as time progresses.

Statistical examinations for the presence of cointegration:

The Augmented Dickey-Fuller (ADF) test is regarded as a statistical technique utilized to ascertain the presence of cointegration. In the Python programming language, achieving this task can be efficiently accomplished by utilizing the stats models library.

In accordance with the principles of trading, it is imperative for pairs to maintain proper functionality that the ratio or spread of stocks undergo periodic changes. In other words, the correlation between the two stocks is necessary.

Merely examining the correlation between the stocks can yield inaccurate outcomes, as the prices of both stocks may rise arbitrarily without any substantive significance. There exists a prevalent belief that two interconnected devices must be in close proximity to one another, and vice versa.

Pair selection

What factors should be considered when selecting stock pairs?

Suppose you possess a substantial portfolio of stocks. The initial phase involves classifying the stock based on market size, sector, daily trading volume, as well as additional variables. Subsequent to the process of division, it is possible to examine the correlation among the securities within each individual grouping.

Correlation facilitates the reduction of pairings into a more feasible subset. After obtaining a limited number of groups, it is advisable to examine the interconnected pairs within each group and subsequently choose the interconnected pairs.

What is the method for selecting currency pairs in the Forex market?

The fundamental concept underpinning the selection of currency pairs in Forex is analogous to that of stocks. We must identify nations with comparable economic foundations.

Presented below are several appropriate pairs.

The currency pairs of EUR / USD and CHF / USD,

The currency pairs of AUD / USD and CAD / USD" or "The foreign exchange rates of AUD / USD and CAD / USD"

The currency pairs being referred to are USD / KRW (United States Dollar / South Korean Won) and USD / HKD (United States Dollar / Hong Kong Dollar).

The duo pertains to the identical economic sphere as the euro, with the Swiss franc being part of the eurozone. One benefit of engaging in currency pair trading within the forex market is that increased liquidity in currencies corresponds to a reduction in trading expenses.

What is the methodology for selecting pairs within the futures market?

Despite identical economic exposure, there is a scarcity of suitable pairings within futures trading. This phenomenon can be attributed to fluctuations in supply and demand. Consequently, future pair selection should not be based solely on economic exposure.

Stop the Loss

You have the option of placing a stop loss order both above and below your predefined threshold.

As an illustration, the prescribed boundary was established as plus/minus 2 standard deviations for the aforementioned position. You have the option to establish a stop loss level that is equivalent to a variance of plus or minus three standard deviations. You have the freedom to close the position once the ratio/spread surpasses this threshold. An alternative strategy entails exiting the position upon reaching a substantial loss in previous trades.

Duration of holding

One may assume the aforementioned role for a duration of one day, one week, or one month, and subsequently terminate their engagement. One can determine the duration for which the position can be maintained by utilizing the concept of half-life. This denotes the duration required for the time series to revert back to its central state. It provides an estimation of the anticipated duration of a specific trade.

When you choose to terminate a position based on time, you will exercise patience until the price reverts to its initial level, subsequently initiating fresh positions.

How To Ensure The Longevity Of Cryptocurrency Investments

Upon embarking on your investment journey, it would be prudent to cultivate an awareness of sustainability. Certain individuals initiate their investment endeavors, only to subsequently experience a decline in resolve; consequently, they become incapable of achieving substantial advancements in the realm of trading or investing after a short period of time. This chapter presents a selection of invaluable recommendations to guarantee the appropriateness of your cryptocurrency investments.

How to maintain the longevity of your cryptocurrency investment

1. Exercise caution

It is imperative for a prudent cryptocurrency investor to remain vigilant at all times due to the inherent volatility of the market. Should you fail to maintain vigilance over your investment, you may one day awaken to the disheartening realization that the coins in your wallets have undergone a significant devaluation. You can enhance your vigilance by consistently reviewing your transactions, thoroughly examining cryptocurrency analyses, and staying informed about each individual coin you utilize.

2. Emphasize the importance of security

You will not be able to achieve enduring investments with an unreliable cryptographic process. Place safety as a foremost concern in all your transactions, thereby enabling the construction of a durable investment portfolio. It is imperative to ensure that all data is properly backed up, employ two-factor authentication, and refrain from disclosing transaction details to any unauthorized individuals or entities.

3. Pay heed to authoritative sources.

There exist individuals with deep knowledge and expertise in the field of cryptocurrencies, who have made significant investments and possess the capability to make reliable forecasts regarding the valuation of coins and their market dynamics. If you heed the counsel of the experts, you will be empowered to anticipate market trends and consequently make astute decisions. Professionals serve as a valuable source of guidance, particularly for individuals who are inexperienced in the field of cryptocurrencies.

4. Exercise patience until the opportune moment comes.

In the realm of cryptocurrency markets, there inherently exists opportune moments. Failure to capitalize on these moments may result in acquiring the appropriate coin during an inopportune timeframe, or inversely. As you increase your trading activity, your familiarity with the timings will grow, allowing you to gain insight into the specific peak periods during which certain coins command the highest sales. Acquiring the appropriate digital currency, on the suitable trading platform, at the opportune moment, and capitalizing on favorable sales transactions is the source of satisfaction for all cryptocurrency investors.

5. Maintain consistency.

Upon embarking on your investment journey, you shall encounter a plethora of obstacles which shall necessitate careful consideration as to whether you ought to persevere or relinquish your endeavors. In order to maintain pace with the journey, it is imperative to consistently engage in the purchase, sale, investment, and trading of your cryptocurrencies. The acquisition of knowledge is facilitated through the maintenance of consistency, thereby fueling the progression of highly skilled investors.

6. Please peruse the text

You are currently engaged in the act of perusing a book as you demonstrate a desire to acquire knowledge. If your intention is to preserve and enhance your investments, it is imperative that you engage in extensive and avid reading. The most astute cryptocurrency investors consistently maintain their edge by remaining abreast of innovative concepts, as they possess a profound comprehension.

7. Persist in your efforts and continue to strive for success.

It is permissible to encounter initial failures in the realm of investment; do not allow such setbacks to hinder your determination along this trajectory. In the face of failure, let steadfast determination guide you to persistently attempt until achieving success. Bear in mind that the cryptocurrency market is characterized by its inherent volatility; nevertheless, it is imperative that you demonstrate unwavering determination in order to maximize the potential returns on your cryptocurrency investment.

Do not simply invest and neglect your assets; it is your duty to diligently monitor and ensure that your investment generates long-term returns. If one adheres strictly to the guidelines laid out in this chapter, they shall undoubtedly achieve success in their investment ventures and cryptocurrency trading. There are immense prospects to anticipate in the forthcoming stages regarding cryptocurrencies. It is imperative that you peruse the subsequent chapter in order to unveil a comprehensive understanding of this subject matter and beyond.

Chapter 7: Investing in Privacy-Focused Blockchains

Have you ever contemplated the rationale behind the proliferation of numerous cryptocurrencies? In concise terms, numerous cryptocurrency initiatives are aiming to tackle a specific application or incorporate a functionality that they perceive to be beyond the capabilities or scope of Bitcoin. For a significant portion of the population, Bitcoin primarily serves as a means of preserving wealth rather than having additional functionalities. Nevertheless, Bitcoin is widely acknowledged as the most steadfast blockchain globally, which has prompted numerous proponents to advocate for the incorporation of crucial attributes such as privacy and smart contract capabilities into the Bitcoin network. An issue arises as the Bitcoin blockchain lacks the capacity to support the volume of decentralized applications constructed on Ethereum, and is incapable of incorporating privacy functionalities similar to Monero due to the potential repercussion of regulatory interventions. However, what if it were possible? In this chapter, I shall elucidate upon the Blockstack cryptocurrency project, which aims to harness the complete capabilities inherent in the Bitcoin blockchain. Blockstack was established by Ryan Shea and Muneeb Ali in 2013 during their time at Princeton University. Ryan is an industrious individual who obtained a Bachelor's degree in the fields of mechanical engineering and computer science, thereby cementing his status as an entrepreneur. In 2018, Ryan departed from Blockstack with the intention of establishing his own venture, the exact name of which has not been revealed. The primary objective of his forthcoming undertaking is to effectively tackle critical challenges that he perceives as the foremost issues confronting mankind, encompassing matters pertaining to cognitive well-being, bioengineering, and the evolution of the employment landscape. Muneeb holds the position of current Chief Executive Officer at Blockstack and, during his tenure at Princeton University, successfully attained a Doctorate in Computer Science. He possesses inherent cypherpunk ideologies and has harbored a profound fascination for the internet ever since his paternal figure first procured a personal computer for him in his early years. Per Muneeb's assertion, our present era can be likened to the nascent stage of the internet's development. This can be attributed to the fact that our interaction with the internet is facilitated through centralized platforms such as Google and Facebook. These entities effectively possess dominion over the digital realm, encompassing both the internet infrastructure and our personal data. In this contemporary digital landscape, it is evident that a select few individuals with significant wealth and influence possess exclusive ownership of all available territories, leaving us devoid of any substantial rights regarding property. This phenomenon has bestowed a significant level of authority upon certain entities, prompting Google to adopt the unofficial motto of "don't be evil" in 2000. This motto was eliminated from Google's code of conduct in the year 2018. Prior to that, Muneeb effectively conveyed the notion that companies such as Google should not possess the authority to engage in unethical behavior from the outset. The 2016 Ted X talk presented by Muneeb had the title "Incapable of Malice," in which he asserted that this expression should constitute the fundamental guiding principle for the future development of the internet. Muneeb's doctoral thesis, entitled "Designing a New Internet: Establishing Trust from Trust," delved into the concept of the forthcoming generation of the internet. In this document, he delineated an architectural design for the internet that fulfills its distinct nature as a comprehensive framework owned by end-users rather than intermediaries. This design would leverage the inherent security offered by the Bitcoin blockchain to ensure clients perpetually retain control over their data. What did he call this design? Blockstack. In contrast to the majority of cryptocurrency initiatives, Blockstack has been in development for nearly eight years, with its initial phase largely dedicated to rigorous evaluation by renowned academics from Princeton and Stanford. When Muneeb released his proposal on Blockstack in 2017, the project had already secured significant funding amounting to millions of dollars and was firmly on track to launching its Initial Coin Offering (ICO). In order to raise awareness of the project, Blockstack organized several gatherings that featured prominent individuals within and beyond the cryptocurrency industry, such as Andreas Antonopoulos and even Edward Snowden. The phrase "Can't be malicious" eventually became Blockstack's authentic aphorism, and in 2019, the Blockstack team went as far as purchasing a prominent advertising space adjacent to Google's headquarters in California to prominently showcase this motto. Presently, we find ourselves on the verge of the concluding phase of the square stacks 2.0 test net, which paves the way for the imminent deployment of its fully operational 2.0 main net. What precisely is the nature of Blockstack and how does it operate? Blockstack is a mission-driven cryptocurrency initiative seeking to establish itself as the premier decentralized computing platform for the forthcoming era of the internet. One may categorize Blockstack as the application layer of the internet. The existing framework currently owned and operated by companies such as Google and Facebook. It constitutes the primary component of the internet that lacks decentralization. Unlike these technology behemoths, Blockstack enables the construction of applications that prioritize user data security and give users full control over their information. To date, Blockstack has been the foundation for approximately 500 applications, one of which was developed by the Blockstack team back in 2016. Currently, Blockstack boasts a substantial user base, with tens of thousands of dedicated users actively engaged on their platform. Additionally, they assert that their ecosystem has successfully onboarded over a million users, including notable individuals such as Tim Berners-Lee, the esteemed inventor of the internet. The distinguishing factor of Blockstack lies in its incorporation of the Bitcoin blockchain for the purposes of security and transaction settlement, despite having its own independent blockchain. In addition, it incorporates BTC as the reserved currency for its proprietary STX token. Blockstack essentially integrates smart contract functionality and security into the Bitcoin network, while maintaining the integrity of the Bitcoin blockchain. It is important to note that Blockstack does not serve as a layer 2 scaling solution for Bitcoin. It constitutes a foundational biological system tethered to Bitcoin's underlying infrastructure. However, might I inquire as to the plausibility of this situation? Let us commence from the beginning. Blockstack employs a sophisticated consensus mechanism known as Proof of Transfer (POX). POX consists

Comprising two assemblies: excavators and colocators. This statement may appear peculiar; however, it is worth noting that excavators do not engage in any form of mining. Taking everything into account, they propose transferring Bitcoin, obtained through the process of mining on the Bitcoin blockchain, to the Blockstack blockchain, with the aim of successfully mining a block and acquiring STX tokens. The likelihood of being selected to mine a square is somewhat variable and somewhat dependent on the amount of Bitcoin that you have submitted. A new Blockstack block is generated concurrently with each new Bitcoin block, and the distribution of STX tokens adheres to a similar protocol as that of Bitcoins. In the POX ecosystem, STX token holders have the opportunity to participate in a 10-day locking mechanism, wherein they entrust their tokens. This allows them to receive a portion of Bitcoin rewards granted by miners as an incentive for securing the network. A minimum of 94,000 STX tokens is required for this purpose, and the Bitcoin rewards obtained are also commensurate with the stakers. All the individual traits and situational data associated with said character. This client persona is leveraged to interact with all the applications within the Blockstack ecosystem. This suggests that there is no requirement for creating a new login and password every time you attempt to access an application. The Blockstack blockchain is intricately linked to the Bitcoin blockchain, signifying that any alterations made to user identities or wallet balances on the Blockstack blockchain can be authenticated using the Bitcoin blockchain. Moreover, this also encompasses the inclusion of intelligent contracts within Blockstack, constructed using a unique programming language known as Clarity, which has been developed and rigorously tested by the Blockstack team in collaboration with

Algorand's team. However, what considerations need to be made regarding the entirety of the data that is not currently maintained on the Blockstack blockchain? Instead of incorporating the common practice seen in most cryptocurrency projects where user data is stored on a blockchain, Blockstack employs the Gaia storage system to store any data generated by users during their interactions with applications developed on the Blockstack platform. Despite the fact that Gaia makes use of commercial cloud storage providers such as Azure and Amazon, the access to the data stored within the platform is governed by Blockstack users. If you have adequate computing power and storage resources available, you have the option to store your own data should you choose not to rely on any of these predetermined distributed storage providers. However, may I inquire about the role of the STX token within this context? STX serves as the indigenous digital currency token of Blockstack. It is advisable to register digital assets for the Blockstack blockchain. This encompasses customer personas and intelligent contracts. In view of all factors, it can be concluded that STX is not truly a deflationary cryptocurrency. This is because the STX tokens that miners earn are compensated through inflation, however, the STX's halving schedule indicates that this inflation is expected to decrease from 0.8% annually to less than 1% after the final halving occurs. Blockstack's three division cycles will mirror those of Bitcoin and are outlined as follows. During the first four years, each square mined on the block stack will provide a miner with a compensation of 1,000 STX tokens. After the initial distribution, the award will decrease successively to 500 STX, then to 250 STX, and finally to 125 STX, depending on the amount of STX stacked, relative to different parameters.

The Blockstack blockchain retains the perpetuity of client rewards by accommodating an unending succession of blocks. In contrast to Bitcoin, Blockstack issued 1.3 billion STX tokens at inception and there is no limitation on the total supply. Taking all factors into consideration, it is not anticipated that the overall stock of STX will exceed 2 billion before the year 2050. The exact categorization of the underlying inventory owned by STX may be somewhat puzzling, but approximately 15% of the symbolic stock was allocated to Blockstack's founders and team, while around 30% was assigned to two depositories under the management of the Blockstack group. The remaining portion was distributed during various private and public financing rounds. A considerable quantity of these tokens are subject to verifiably itemized vesting schemes, spanning a duration of two to seven years. Commencing in October 2018, when the initial block was mined and the tokens were disbursed, these vesting plans were implemented. It is noteworthy that Blockstack proactively engaged with regulatory authorities, including the Securities and Exchange

Commission, to ensure full compliance of their STX token sales. Blockstack's initial coin offering (ICO) in 2017 was granted approval by the Securities and Exchange Commission (SEC), making it one of the pioneering ICOs to receive regulatory authorization. The initial coin offering (ICO) garnered approximately 50 million US dollars, while Blockstack managed to accumulate a total funding of around 80 million US dollars through various private and public financing rounds since 2013. The STX token has been in circulation for slightly over a year, yet it has not realized significant value-based transactions. It is currently valued at approximately twenty-five cents, representing a modest two-fold increase from its initial coin offering price of approximately 12 cents. However, the departure of Blockstack's super net is not too distant. When it is deployed, you will essentially have the opportunity to pledge STX in order to earn Bitcoin, a concept that is quite unprecedented in the cryptocurrency realm. Anticipating that the stacking rewards will prove valuable, it is plausible to assert that this will generate significant interest in the STX token. In order to participate as a stacker on the Blockstack blockchain, a possession of 94,000 STX tokens is necessary. The total expenditure, based on current rates, would amount to approximately 23.5 thousand US dollars. The substantial influx of liquidity resulting from this may potentially have the opposite effect if the rewards fail to justify the initial investment in such a highly restrictive sector. Furthermore, regrettably, we will remain uninformed of those measurements until the underlying network becomes operational. If you have an intention to acquire STX, it would be advisable to consider Binance as the most prudent choice. The liquidity of STX on Binance is substantial; nevertheless, it is important to note that the current readiness for withdrawing STX tokens from Binance is lacking. This could potentially be attributed to the imminent advent of the square stack 2.0 blockchain, thereby causing result in a divergence of the blockchain. In any case, when the opportunity arises for you to withdraw your assets, the primary wallet that currently supports the STX token is Blockstack's desktop wallet. It is compatible with both Windows and Mac OS operating systems. Given our close monitoring of the buyer market, many of you will likely benefit from holding onto your STX. What's next for Blockstack? Coincidentally, Blockstack underwent a rebranding in October 2020 and adopted the name Stacks. The primary objective of undertaking this action was to mitigate the confusion arising from the coexistence of the Blockstack project and Blockstack PBC, the technology company headquartered in New York responsible for building Blockstack. Given that this rebranding process is still in progress, I made the decision to retain their previous name in order to maintain clarity and simplicity. I would acknowledge that this rebranding legitimization is quite peculiar, particularly given the fact that

Blockstack PBC underwent a rebranding to Hero Systems PBC in October 2020 as well. This transitional shift to Hero signified a strategic redirection of the organization's focus from nurturing the Blockstack blockchain to developing tools for developers in order to enhance the expansion of Blockstack's existing ecosystem. It also served as a means of connecting the community to broader subjects, such as cryptography, privacy, and digital ownership. This aligns with the venture's overarching goal of enabling on-anchor voting for Blockstack and potentially granting the entire ecosystem to STX token holders. As far as the progression of the Blockstack test net rollout is concerned, we are currently in the third phase out of four. It will underscore the integration with their Bitcoin test network, which represents the final phase before their full mainnet launch, scheduled to take place by the beginning of 2021. In 2021, the focus will primarily be directed towards the development of the Blockstack ecosystem through the utilization of incentives and Blockstack's application mining initiative. Therefore, application mining entails compensating developers who are capable of crafting superior applications as assessed by Blockstack users. Blockstack has made a successful endeavor in the past to achieve this objective, resulting in the rapid development of numerous applications. I anticipate that the upcoming phase of application mining will yield superior results, primarily due to the implementation of DeFi protocols specifically designed for the Bitcoin blockchain. I must assert that it is rare to encounter an endeavor that exhibits such fervent devotion to the fundamental principles and ideals of Bitcoin. Blockstack represents the embodiment of a desire shared by numerous proponents of Bitcoin maximalism—to extend smart contract functionality and enhance the security of the Bitcoin blockchain. Blockstack achieves this by connecting its proprietary blockchain to Bitcoin's blockchain, leveraging a unique consensus mechanism known as Proof of Transfer. Under this system, miners deposit Bitcoin onto the network to mine blocks and earn STX tokens, while stakeholders lock up their STX tokens to receive the Bitcoin deposited by miners as a reward for securing the network. Blockstack enables users to seamlessly engage with applications within the Blockstack ecosystem.

Within the framework of the Blockstack blockchain, a virtual persona is employed to engage with the surroundings. As Blockstack's blockchain is anchored to the Bitcoin network, any modifications made to the Blockstack blockchain can also be verified on the Bitcoin blockchain. Most importantly, Blockstack empowers users to regain command over their data through the implementation of the Gaia storage system. This system offers users the option to securely store their data either on a trusted cloud service provider or using their own physical apparatus. Clients exercise exclusive authority over the access to this information at all times and determine the instances when applications or other entities on Blockstack are permitted to view it. With the imminent launch of Blockstack, there are strong indications for a positive outlook on the project and its associated local STX token. In any case, all of this seems to hinge upon a fundamental variable, which is whether or not Bitcoin holders will indeed partake as miners on the Blockstack blockchain. I express a degree of skepticism, taking into account the requirement of effectively converting Bitcoin into STX tokens. I must express my hesitancy in parting with my Bitcoins, especially considering that we are currently at the onset of what has the potential to be the most significant surge in Bitcoin's history. The potential value of those STX mining rewards must be significant enough to justify diverging from my Bitcoin holdings, even if I could utilize those intellectual STX tokens to acquire even more Bitcoin, provided that the rewards meet expectations. As we are currently unaware of the nature of those rewards, we shall have to temporarily suspend our progress and await further clarification.

Factors To Consider Prior To Investing In Bitcoin

1. Acquire Fundamental Knowledge Initially

Initially, it would be advisable to acquire foundational knowledge in order to gain a more comprehensive understanding of the process involved in purchasing and selling Bitcoin. Furthermore, it would be advisable to peruse reviews of prominent Bitcoin exchanges in order to identify the optimal platform.

Similar to other forms of financial investments, it may be prudent to seek methods to safeguard your investment. Ensure the security of your assets from fraudulent individuals and cyber threats. Ultimately, the paramount factor in any form of investment is the assurance of security.

2. Take into account the Market Capitalization.

It would not be prudent to base this decision solely on the price of the coin. Nevertheless, the value of the cryptocurrency can only be deemed valid when taking into account the quantity currently in circulation.

If you are interested in acquiring Bitcoin, it is advisable not to overly fixate on the present valuation of the currency. Alternatively, it would be prudent to consider the overall market capitalization.

3. Allocate resources towards investing in Bitcoin rather than engaging in Bitcoin mining.

The Bitcoin mining industry is rapidly gaining popularity. Initially, it was not particularly arduous to acquire Bitcoin through the deciphering of cryptographic puzzles. Subsequently, it became feasible to mine Bitcoin exclusively in specialized data centers.

These facilities are comprised of various machinery specifically engineered for the purpose of extracting Bitcoin. Presently, should one wish to construct a mining center within the confines of their own residence, it is possible that one may need to allocate a substantial sum of several million dollars. Therefore, it would be advisable to allocate funds towards Bitcoin investments.

4. Expand the scope of your investment portfolio

Novice investors in Bitcoin often exhibit a transient enthusiasm for cryptocurrencies. Indeed, Bitcoin presents the opportunity to mitigate investment risk by allowing for diversification. If one makes smart investments in cryptocurrency, they can reap the identical benefits as those achieved through investing in Forex. You simply need to develop a robust risk management strategy.

Alternatively, it may not be advisable to concentrate all of your resources in a single entity. Therefore, it would be advisable to consider investing in additional cryptocurrencies.

5. Establish specific objectives

Given that Bitcoin is a nascent market, determining the optimal timing for trading your Bitcoin might prove to be challenging. The value of Bitcoin exhibits significant volatility, necessitating the establishment of precise profit and loss targets.

It would be ill-advised to base your investment decisions solely on emotional factors. Implementing strategic decisions can aid in reducing losses and achieving substantial advancement.

To summarize, we advise adhering to the recommendations provided in this article if you intend to invest in Bitcoin. This will assist you in making prudent decisions and ensuring your safety simultaneously. Please ensure that you steer clear of the typical errors associated with managing this enterprise.

The Existing Condition Of The Market

The Near Future

In the forthcoming year, the trading of cryptocurrencies is poised to persist in a manner akin to its current trajectory. Bitcoin will maintain its leadership position in the market. Nevertheless, it is the currencies with comparatively smaller market capitalizations that possess the greatest likelihood of substantial growth and expansion. Specifically, there is a growing tendency within the market to favor currencies that are supported by reputable corporations and endorsed by well-known individuals. For instance, XRP is currently poised for another increment in its price, potentially recouping a portion of its value from the year 2017.

We anticipate further escalations in pricing akin to those observed in 2017. Once prices begin to reach their maximum levels once again, it is anticipated that traders hailing from various nations will converge on the market. The collective mindset of the group will persist in driving prices upwards, surpassing even the previously established price limits.

The subsequent surge in prices can potentially be instigated by various factors:

Positive Government Policies

Amidst the 2017 trading frenzy, it became imperative for governments to expeditiously take measures to safeguard their citizens from the inherent risks associated with cryptocurrency trading. This gave rise to a series of myopic strategies that led to the significant downturn observed in the initial months of 2018.

Nevertheless, banks and other financial institutions are endeavoring to acquire adeptness in leveraging blockchain technology within their operational frameworks. If the pioneering banks successfully identify favorable applications for this technology, it is highly likely that other smaller banks will emulate their approach. Consequently, these additional financial institutions will engage in consultations with cryptocurrency developers to explore the incorporation of blockchain technology into their operational framework.

The involvement of banks and other financial institutions in research pertaining to cryptocurrencies will contribute to bolstering the credibility of cryptocurrencies in the eyes of governments worldwide. Significant advancements in the realm of cryptocurrencies within the financial sector are anticipated to occur either towards the latter part of 2018 or during the course of 2019. Nevertheless, there is no assurance that this outcome will occur.

Collaboration with various sectors

Reports regarding the favorable adoption outcomes of cryptocurrencies will engender a surge in their market valuations. Currently, solely the investment industry and the financial sector demonstrate a motivation to employ cryptocurrencies. Nevertheless, scholars across a multitude of academic disciplines are actively investigating alternative implementations of blockchain technology.

Ethereum stands out as the most promising cryptocurrency poised to expand beyond the realm of investment and make significant inroads within the financial sector. Its DAPP concept is attracting developers from around the world, thereby increasing the value of Ether. Nevertheless, among the multitude of DAPPs that are set to be developed, a staggering majority of over 90% are expected to face failure. This has been observed to hold true in the domains of website and app development in the past, and it is anticipated to yield identical results in the case of Ethereum DAPPs.

The inquiry would pertain to whether the top 10% of the DAPPs created would suffice in garnering consumer backing for the Ethereum network. This outcome will be contingent upon the nature of the applications that will be created.

Escalated utilization beyond conventional currencies in outdoor settings

Cryptocurrencies have flourished as financial assets. Indeed, this is presently its sole significant purpose. In the event that a sole cryptocurrency among the multitude available in the market manages to establish itself as a functional medium of exchange, it has the potential to significantly enhance the value of other cryptocurrencies in circulation as well as future promising Initial Coin Offerings (ICOs).

According to the preceding chapters, only a select few cryptocurrencies possess viable potential to establish themselves as genuine currencies. Numerous specialists maintain the view that such occurrence remains plausible as an industry of interest fully adopts a cryptocurrency as its predominant means of transaction. One instance of this can be seen in the acceptance of Bitcoin by clandestine online platforms as their preferred mode of transaction.

Industries dealing with digital products are inclined to be more receptive to adopting cryptocurrency as a medium of exchange. These kinds of products and services are not solely reliant on tangible materials found in the physical realm. Exemplary content-based products such as audiobooks, videos, and downloadable software do not necessitate tangible resources in their composition. They have the capability to be promptly sold and delivered to the user, who can then utilize cryptocurrency as a means of transaction.

Additionally, certain scholars are conducting investigations into the potential utility of blockchain technology as a means to combat piracy. Digital products that are acquired have the capability to be registered onto a blockchain utilizing unique identification codes. Subsequently, this identification code could be employed to authenticate individuals' possession of these digital commodities.

In addition to the technology sector, scholars are actively investigating alternative implementations for cryptocurrency and blockchain technology. Some individuals are exploring the potential of employing it as a worldwide repository for land registration, whereas others are assessing its viability for utilization in sectors such as education, sales, and various other industries.

The Distant Future

It is undeniable that the future of cryptocurrency remains uncertain. In order for them to achieve long-term success, it is imperative that their stated use cases are actualized. Bitcoin is primarily intended to supplant cash as the predominant means of transacting on the internet. The achievement of this use case will determine the success of Bitcoin. In the event that it does not materialize, there remains a potential for bitcoin to persevere as a viable investment asset. Nevertheless, should individuals come to hold the belief that the foremost purpose of a monetary unit is unachievable, unquestionably, said currency will gradually forfeit its pertinence. Subsequently, this will result in the devaluation of its price.

Should you decide to engage in the cryptocurrency market, it is imperative that you remain cognizant of the latest updates surrounding the progression of the cryptocurrencies in which you are involved. Furthermore, during the selection process, ensure that you opt for currencies that have the utmost potential for success in actualizing their designated purposes.

Understanding Blockchain Technology

If you possess some familiarity with cryptocurrencies, it is likely that you have come across references to the blockchain, a technological framework that underpins Bitcoin and numerous other digital currencies. In addition to this commonly accepted explanation, have you acquired substantial knowledge regarding the true nature and mechanics of the blockchain? Are you acquainted with the functioning mechanisms?

The current manifestation of the blockchain is the innovative creation of Satoshi Nakamoto, the anonymous progenitor of Bitcoin. Put simply, the blockchain can be characterized as an immutable, decentralized, and public ledger that maintains a record of transactions. To put it differently, the blockchain can be described as an open registry wherein once an entry is recorded, it becomes unchangeable.

Furthermore, it exhibits a decentralized structure. What does this mean?

In essence, decentralization entails the absence of a central governing body vested with the authority to exercise decision-making power. Conversely, the assignment of this duty is bestowed upon every member within the organization. The accountability for this task lies with each and every computer comprising the network in question. Henceforth, it is impossible for any single entity to exert regulatory control over the blockchain. On the contrary, the members establish interpersonal connections by adhering to universally applicable mathematical principles. In order to establish the authenticity of a decision or transaction, unanimous consensus among all networked computers is imperative. In order to elucidate the concept of decentralization, I will employ an illustrative exemplification.

Conventionally, in the context of collaborative document creation, it was customary for one individual to undertake the initial work on the document and subsequently transmit it to the other party for the purpose of incorporating their respective revisions into it. In this particular situation, the initial individual is unable to perceive the modifications implemented by the second individual until a copy of the revised document is dispatched back. The initial individual would also be required to await the receipt of the revised document before proceeding with any subsequent modifications. Ultimately, the responsibility for determining the correct version would rest with a single individual. Nonetheless, in the event that the two individuals were to employ the Google Docs software, they would both have simultaneous access to the document. Both individuals would have the ability to implement modifications simultaneously, thereby ensuring that the most updated iteration of the document is readily accessible to both parties concurrently.

The process of submitting the document for alterations can be likened to the functioning of contemporary databases. This is the protocol employed by financial institutions for the purpose of managing and facilitating monetary balances and transactions. Access is temporarily restricted on one side, the transfer is executed, and subsequently access is reinstated. In contrast, the blockchain can be likened to the Google Doc platform, wherein all participants possess an identical copy of the public ledger throughout the entire duration. However, in contrast to its sharing between two individuals, the blockchain is dispersed across multiple stakeholders. Nevertheless, the blockchain further elevates this concept. Rather than assigning the task of deciding the correct version of the document to one individual, it is imperative that all individuals with access to the document collectively reach a consensus on the accurate version. By engaging in this practice, the blockchain achieves a level of resilience that mirrors the robustness found in the internet. It lacks the potential for individual control and is devoid of any singular failure point.

Similar to the Google Doc application, the blockchain perpetually maintains a state of consensus. It performs periodic self-assessment and updates itself automatically to the most current version across all nodes. The collection of transactions that occur between each automated update is referred to as a block. The perpetual state of agreement yields two consequences. Initially, it facilitates transparency as the most up-to-date iteration of the database is perceptible to all individuals connected within the network. Furthermore, it signifies the resilience of the blockchain against any forms of tampering or corruption. Manipulating the blockchain would entail acquiring dominance over a significant portion of the computational nodes within the network. Although the notion appears theoretically feasible, its practical realization is highly improbable due to the substantial computational resources that would be required. Assuming control over the blockchain would inevitably lead to the depreciation of the cryptocurrencies' worth.

A System of Nodal Connections

The blockchain is composed of a distributed network of computers commonly referred to as nodes. These computers operate the blockchain protocol, enabling them to engage in message transmission and reception with one another. Nodes have the option to join the network on a voluntary basis. Upon the initiation of a new node's connection to the network, it promptly undertakes the task of acquiring the most up-to-date iteration of the blockchain. The aforementioned nodes hold a significant role within each and every blockchain network. Upon the inclusion of a node into the network, it assumes the role of a co-administrator on the network. It is entrusted with the duty of aiding in the authentication of each and every transaction occurring on the blockchain. Upon verification, the node proceeds to append the transaction to a block. This process continues until a block reaches its culmination, at which point the node proceeds to incorporate it into the blockchain. The likelihood of receiving newly generated coins serves as a motivating factor for the nodes to carry out these administrative responsibilities within the blockchain network.

When a sender initiates a transfer of coins to another recipient, the nodes meticulously examine the transaction data to verify the authenticity and legitimacy of the transfer. It conducts a comparative analysis between the transaction data and its own iteration of the blockchain to validate that the coins have not been subject to double spending. Should the node determine that the transaction data is invalid, it will promptly decline the transaction. In addition, it refuses any subsequent correspondence with the node that transmitted the transaction. Nodes establish a relationship with other nodes on the network that is not reliant on trust. Hence, in the event that one node transmits erroneous data to the remaining nodes, they promptly sever communication with said node and enforce its expulsion from the network.

Notwithstanding, should the node determine the legitimacy of the transaction data, it shall proceed to relay said transaction to miners. Miners aggregate transactions in a sequential manner to generate blocks. After the completion of a block, it is subsequently returned to the nodes for the purpose of verification. All validation is conducted solely by nodes, as they are inherently incapable of disseminating erroneous information. After the nodes have verified the authenticity of a block, they are then able to append it to the blockchain.

The efficacy of blockchain technology is grounded on the subsequent three fundamental technologies:

Private Key Cryptography

The blockchain enables individuals to conduct internet-based transactions without reliance on a trusted intermediary. Nevertheless, in order to ensure the safety and security of the transaction, a certain level of trust must be established. In the realm of the internet, trust can be distilled to two essential components – the verification of identity, or authentication, and the verification of permissions, known as authorization. In essence, it is necessary to establish a means of corroborating individuals' true identities and ascertaining their authorization for their intended actions.

When considering blockchain technology, trust is forged through the implementation of private key cryptography. Cryptography utilizes mathematical principles to encode information into a confidential cipher that remains beyond the reach of unauthorized individuals. In order to obtain access to the information, one will require a decryption key.

A cryptocurrency transaction essentially entails the transmission of encrypted information from one individual to another. Whenever an individual undertakes a transaction on the blockchain, said transaction undergoes encryption via the utilization of cryptographic keys. For each individual transaction, a pair of mathematically correlated keys, namely a public key in conjunction with a private key, are generated. In order to facilitate an encrypted transaction, it is essential to possess the recipient's public key. In order to decipher the transaction, possession of the private key is imperative. The private key serves as the unique identifier of the cryptocurrency wallet, enabling the transmission of encrypted data (in the form of crypto coins) to the wallet's rightful owner. Nevertheless, in order to obtain the coins, the owner must decrypt the data by employing their private key. The possession of the private key serves as proof of ownership of the wallet address. The private key additionally serves as verification of your authorization to engage in transactions, signifying that you possess adequate coins for conducting such transactions. By means of the private key, the blockchain validates legitimacy and authorization, thus resolving the matter of trust.

A Distributed Network

In order for the blockchain to achieve efficacy, authentication and authorization alone prove insufficient. Furthermore, it is imperative to establish a decentralized peer-to-peer network. This network effectively addresses the matter of security and record-keeping. In order for transactions to be deemed valid, they must undergo confirmation by the entire network. This phenomenon can be elucidated through the application of a renowned conceptual exercise commonly referred to as the 'if a tree falls in the forest'. Nevertheless, our contemplative exercise will be subtly modified.

In the event of a tree toppling within a wooded area, with the presence of two functioning cameras recording the incident, we can confidently ascertain the veracity of the tree's descent, as there exists substantive visual documentation of the occurrence. Nevertheless, in the event that one camera documented the descent of the tree, while the other failed to do so, we are unable to establish with certainty the veracity of the tree's collapse. This constitutes the underlying principle behind the intrinsic worth of the blockchain network. The network consists of the cameras in our analogy. In the event that the nodes come to a unanimous agreement regarding the occurrence of the event at a specific moment, there exists a state of certainty regarding the event's actuality. In order for a transaction to be verified as legitimate, a consensus among the majority of the nodes must be reached, affirming the occurrence of the transaction. Nevertheless, rather than employing cameras, the nodes utilize mathematical puzzles for the purpose of validation.

When the amalgamation of private key cryptography and the distributed network occurs, it results in an augmentation of efficacy within the blockchain. An individual, employing their private key as means of establishing genuineness and authorization, declares to the network their intention to carry out a transaction, wherein the entire network diligently observes and verifies the occurrence of said transaction.

A motivating factor for the enhancement of security measures and meticulous record-keeping

Though the integration of private key cryptography and a distributed network may appear impervious, it harbors a singular vulnerability. What is the rationale behind the nodes exercising patience to observe and verify the occurrence of a transaction? In other words, how does the network effectively allure nodes to verify transactions and thereby fortify the network's security? This is the point at which mining becomes relevant. The nodes receive newly generated coins as a reward for executing administrative functions and upholding network security. The nodes' pursuit of personal benefit is leveraged for the betterment of the public.

www.ingramcontent.com/pod-product-compliance
Lightning Source LLC
Chambersburg PA
CBHW050253120526
44590CB00016B/2334